First Edition
ISBN: 978-1-958189-50-4
Opossum Hollow
Nature's Nighttime Heroes and Small-Town Celebrities
Written by **F. J. Patterson**

To B.F

The woman who sparked my love for programming and shared with me the wonder of possums.

Without your inspiration, this book would never have been imagined, let alone written.

Thank you for planting the seed that grew into this adventure.

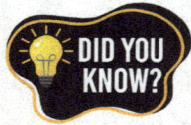

First things first—guess what? I'm a **marsupial!** That means I carry my babies in a pouch, kinda like a kangaroo! Only mines a **vertical** pouch

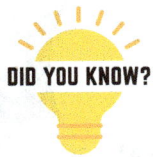

I have a big family! I carry my
babies—called **joeys**—in my pouch
to keep them safe and warm.
We can have about **13 babies** in one
litter—wow, that's a lot of little
joeys!

This is one of my babies **Noah**. Can you say hi to him?
Hi, friends! **Noah** squeaks.

We possums are **nocturnal**, which means we sleep during the day and come out when the moon is up. The night is our playground!

See my long tail?
It's **prehensile**—that means I can grab things with it, like tree branches!
I call it my built-in jungle gym rope!

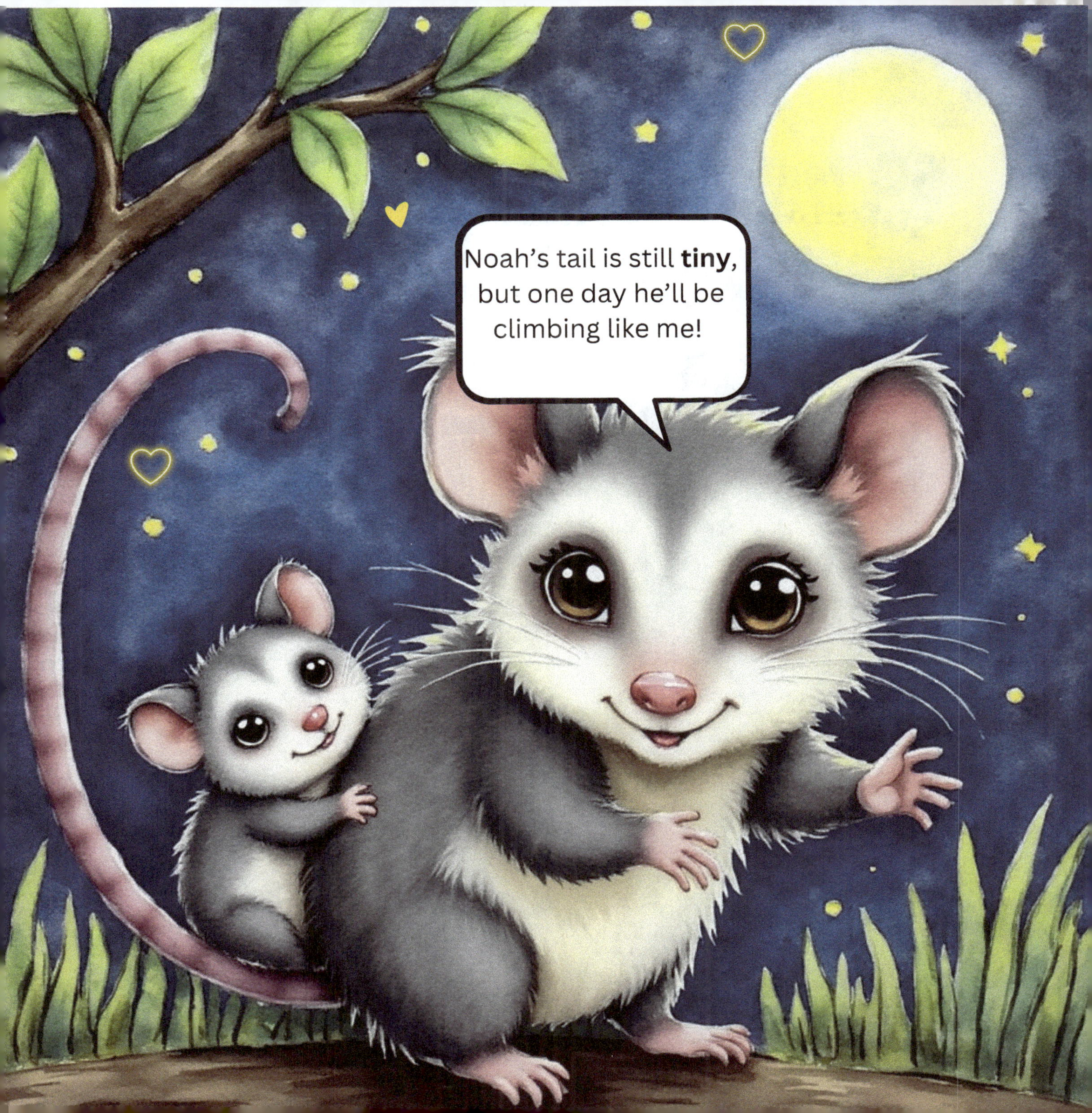
Noah's tail is still **tiny**, but one day he'll be climbing like me!

Berries? Yes!

Bugs? Yum!

Leftover snacks? You betcha!

Wanna hear something cool?

We don't get sick from lots of things
even **snake bites** and **germs!**
Scientists think we're so cool, they study us to help make **medicines** for
people!

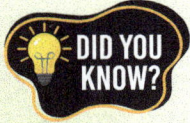

Noah and I come from an ancient family. Fossils show possums have been around since the time of the dinosaurs!

Sometimes, when I get really scared...
I do something super silly!
I **play dead**! 😲💤
It's called **"playing possum."**

I go all stiff, stick out my tongue,
and even make a **stinky smell!**

That way, animals think I'm dead and leave me alone.
Pretty smart, right?
It helps keep me safe!

People think we’re so special, they throw **festivals** just for us!
Wanna hear about some?

In **Wausau, Florida**, we're royalty—they call it the **Possum Capital of the World!** They even crown a Possum King and Queen! 👑

Over in Cumberland, Kentucky, there's **Possum Fest**—with games, crafts, and yummy treats.

Indiana celebrates **Possum' Palooza,** where families gather to cheer for us possums!

And don't forget **Texas**! Their **Possum Fest** is packed with dancing, food, and good ol' fun. **Yeehaw!**
Ain't we just the life of the party?

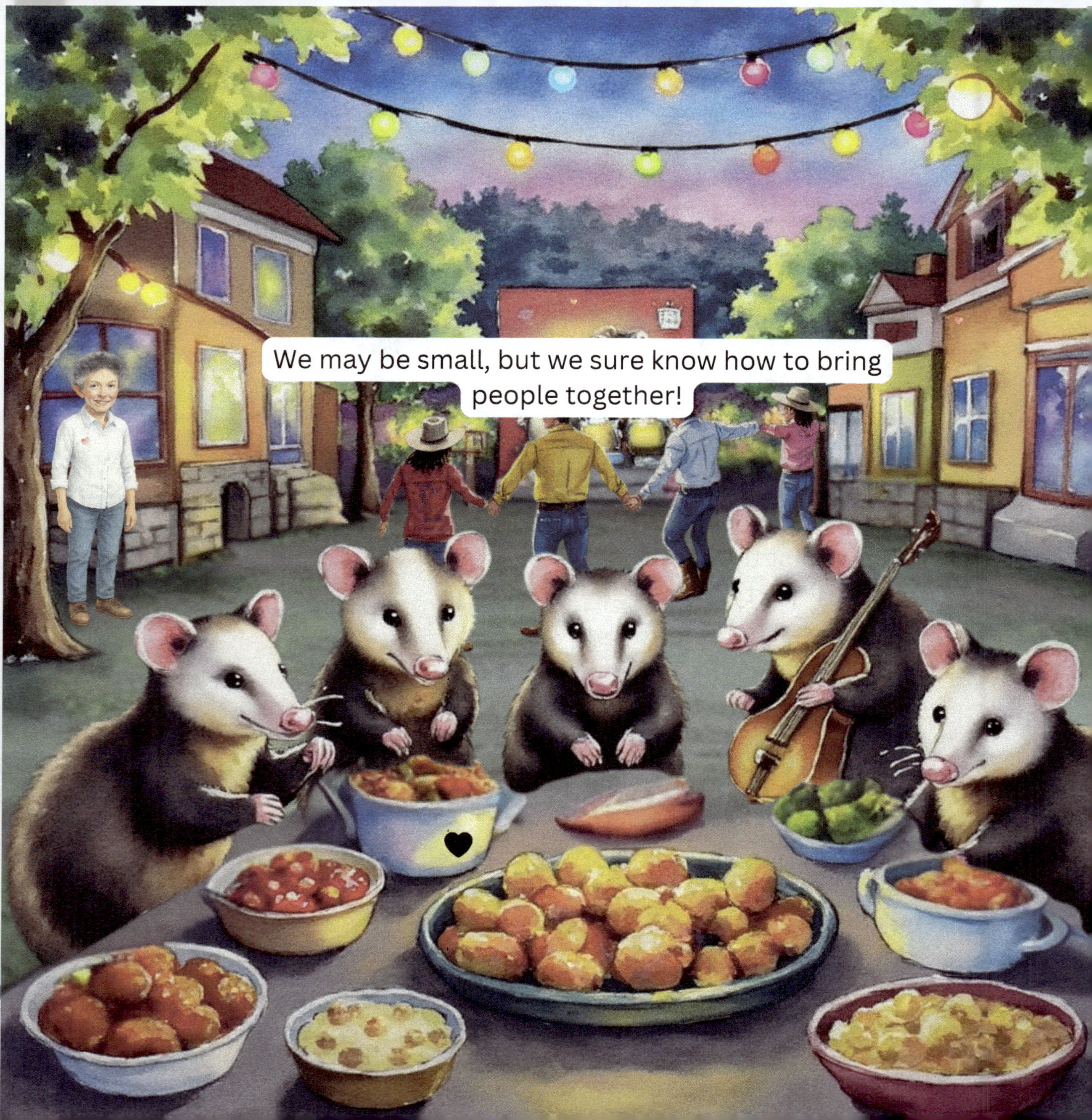
We may be small, but we sure know how to bring people together!

Well, friends, Noah and I are getting sleepy.
The sun is rising, and it’s time to curl up tight.
Thanks for joining us on our nighttime adventure!
See you next time

Special Bonus

Opossums love playing hide and seek. Every picture has one or more heart's hidden within the page. How many can you find?

www.ingramcontent.com/pod-product-compliance
Lightning Source LLC
Chambersburg PA
CBHW061827260326
41914CB00005B/899